SPEAKING WIRI WIRI

SPEAKING WIRI WIRI

poems by

Dan Vera

Red Hen Press | *Pasadena, CA*

Book design and layout by Skyler Schulze

Library of Congress Cataloging-in-Publication Data

Vera, Dan.
  [Poems. Selections]
  Speaking Wiri Wiri : poems / by Dan Vera.—First edition.
     pages cm
  Winner of the inaugural Letras Latinas/Red Hen Poetry Prize.
  ISBN 978-1-59709-274-6
  I. Title.
  PS3622.E69S64 2013
  811'.6—dc23
                          2012044239

The National Endowment for the Arts, the Los Angeles County Arts Commission, the Los Angeles Department of Cultural Affairs, the City of Pasadena Cultural Affairs Division, Sony Pictures Entertainment, and the Dwight Stuart Youth Fund partially support Red Hen Press.

First Edition
Published by Red Hen Press
www.redhen.org

Acknowledgments

Poems in the manuscript have appeared in the following journals and anthologies (sometimes in different versions or under different titles):

Beltway Poetry Quarterly, "Artifact" and "Purifying America's Textbooks of Ethnic Studies"; *Divining Divas: 100 Gay Men on their Muses*, "All Oranges and Bananas Now"; *Gargoyle*, "Lago de Mil Ojos" and "Nabokov Visits the Smithsonian"; *Little Patuxent Review*, "Mr. Guzman Makes a Fool of Himself"; *Naugatuck River Review*, "How La Lupe Defeated the Alien Invasion of 1969"; *The Notre Dame Review*, "Monarch Butterfly" and "Tower of Babel"; and *Undefined*, "The Perils of the Monumental."

The writing of many of these poems was supported by a fellowship from the Virginia Center for the Creative Arts. I'm also grateful for the support of Francisco Aragon and the visionary lights of Letras Latinas at the University of Notre Dame; and for the continued familial and writerly kinship of friends and colleagues like Michael Gushue, Kim Roberts, Teri Cross Davis, Abby Beckel, Sarah Browning, Regie Cabico, Susan Scheid, and Joe Ross. They remind me of how lucky I am to be a writer living in a collaborative community of peers like Washington, DC. I am thankful to my parents and family and most of all to my lover and fere, Peter.

In the poem, "Nabokov Visits the Smithsonian," the lines, "it will transcend its dust" and "wide open on its pin" are taken from Vladimir Nabokov's "On Discovering a Butterfly."

Contents

3. The Trouble with Memory

4. The Memory of the Tongue

5. The Guide to Imaginary Monuments

Dan Vera is a poet haunted by memory, haunted by place, haunted by words. Of course, these are the wellsprings of poetry in general, but in Vera's case there is the added complication of having been born to Cuban parents in South Texas, a bastion of Mexican-American culture where *cubanidad* (so prevalent in Miami) might be as rare as Turkishness. Nonetheless, it is clear that both his father and mother insisted on preserving the memory of their Caribbean homeland, at times with somber consequences, yet just as often with hilarious results, as in the poem "Tower of Babel" where his father requests *menudo* (change) for a five-dollar bill at a Dallas restaurant, but the Mexican owner instead thinks he wants five dollars' worth of tripe soup.

This is not the only word that would cause such comical miscommunication. I can easily see Vera writing another Babelian poem on *tortilla*, which to Cubans (and Spaniards) means a thick potato omelet, often eaten as a sandwich (*bocadillo* in Spain), though the Cuban *pan con tortilla* would, of course, make no sense whatsoever to Mexicans (or Americans, for that matter). I recall Winston Churchill's wry comment that "Britain and America are two nations divided by a common language." The same can be said of Spanish, no doubt, but Vera adopts a more nuanced approach, as in "Wiri Wiri" (meaning gibberish, a phrase invented by his humorous father) where the poet asserts that language both "holds us together" and "holds us apart," thereby acknowledging the fraught relationship between language and culture.

It must be said, however, that Vera, unlike his more alienated parents, does feel an intrinsic connection to Mexican culture. For example, his beautiful poem "Monarch Butterfly" gives homage to the Aztecs, as well as to Cuba's Guanahacabibes, cave dwellers who vanished soon after the Spanish conquest. Vera clearly feels a sense of present kinship with these autochthonous Americans, even if for most Cubans, the Taínos, who survived in *encomiendas* (reservations) well into the eighteenth century, belong to a quaint, forgotten past. As a poet driven to reconstruct the fragments of memory, just as an archeologist rebuilds ancient ruins, Vera knows that any possible reconnection to the past depends on a prescient understanding of the copious interplay between language and culture, made more lush still by the mediation of his Romantic imagination.

For example, the poem "Gocha," named after a Cuban woman in the poet's past, lovingly recounts how this exile taught him "the flowers of her memory / blue *fausto* and *azulejo, majagua* and *flamboyán*. / In every garden she planted *camelia*, / tenacious reminder of all she left behind." Gocha's lesson is not merely a signpost or marker on the poet's journey into cultural memory, but rather triggers a powerful self-transformation: "I have taken this new land inside of me / bluebonnet, western bluebell, heat's chicory / and plant *camelia* in my garden / to remind me of the geographies that preceded me." I perceive the character Gocha, whether real or imagined or both, as a kind of seer, perhaps even a shaman, who guides the poet into a past that cannot actually be recollected (the poet has never been to Cuba) but imaginatively experienced in the body as a mythic garden that contains flowers representing Vera's bilingual, bicultural makeup.

I would add that the poet engages in this reconstruction of memory, this rebuilding of *imaginary monuments*, with a profound awareness of his parents' "desire and despair" brought about by their exilic condition. It is a heavy responsibility to live in one's parents' past, no doubt, especially when this past makes one feel inadequate and incomplete. In "Small Shame Blues," the poet, as a second-generation Cuban American, confesses that he "live[s] with the small shame / which resides in the absences of [his] speech / as [he] pause[s] to search for the word in Spanish." He belongs to the generation that "goes searching for [names] sifting through dust / through dictionaries of the obscure and archaic / for syllables that still tremble with the older meanings" ("How the Land Longs to Be Loved"). Another person would have avoided this agonistic search for his roots (both linguistically and culturally), but Vera chose instead to persevere in connecting with his ancestral homeland, and I can only explain this doggedness as the result of a deep familial bond, an emotional debt that has to be repaid with poetry and poetry alone.

—Orlando Ricardo Menes

And what do thought and memory lead to? . . .

—Conrad Aiken

I

The Trouble with Language

let us go down, and there confound their language,
that they may not understand one another's speech.

Genesis 11:7

Kvetch

As my Gentile tongue screws up that perfect Yiddish sound,
Kim complains we have no right to a word if it's mispronounced.

I tell her *cry me the River Grande River*
and recite the litany of the beautiful made bland.

They made *La Jolla*, merely jolly
and drove the angels right out of *Los Angeles*.

They even made *La Virgen* into *What a loop*.
And then I learn it's from the Arabic

Guadalupe from *wadi lupus*
for *the valley where wolves reside.*

Folded up and carried over oceans and epochs,
syllable reminders of our grandmothers' voices

that reside inside the hollow of the ear
till they come cascading miraculous

out of a stranger's mouth,
mangled accents and twisted tenses all.

Wiri Wiri

The language holds us together.
How you are bathed in it
till you tire and run
or are pushed away from the tongue
by parents who'd spare you the hurdles they jumped.

The language pulls us apart.
How we are bathed in it
made to never forget,
reprimanded for not speaking it
by parents who would not be left behind.

¡En esta casa se habla Español!
¡No se habla el wiri wiri!
Demands for the sounds
from that singular place
with its undeniable song.

I Know You Little Codfish

The phrases of our fathers
creep up as we grow older
providing the voice-over
to our daily life.

¡Te conozco bacalao!
when we are fooled by the world,
¡Ave Maria Puríssima!
when we are left to exclamate.

These words surprise us
in the sea of our daily English,
appear like flotsam from a shipwreck
long believed to be submerged.

They reveal memory to be the master
of a treasure more profound
than any English we may have mastered.

Tower of Babel

Exegesis of a funny story:
in which my father asks for change
change being *menudo* for Cubans
menudo being tripe soup for Mexicans.

It is 1966 in Dallas, Texas
my father makes his request
to the owner of a Mexican restaurant

Who is delighted to comply
and asks how much *menudo* he'd like.
My father replies *five-dollars worth*.

This is 1966 and the owner asks
if my father brought a container
to carry home five-dollars worth.

Considering it a joke
my father smiles and replies
I'll carry it in my hand.

Thinking of the gallons
the owner is not amused
and insists on a container.

Then the shouting commences
as neither man can be convinced
he is not dealing with an idiot.

My father keeps pointing to his palm
while the owner makes the shape of a vessel
and they grow angrier with each other.

Finally one of my father's friends
rescues him from the exchange
takes him aside and explains the difference.

and with these words
the woman in the checkout welcomes me
not in the second language I learned
so long ago I do not remember not knowing it
but in the language of my parents.

In my mind there is a historical marker
outside this corner bodega
in Chicago's Puerto Rican neighborhood
where I was expected to know
and speak the Spanish language
the very moment in my own history
when a stranger assumed I belonged.

At first I am shocked
then delight in the ability to reply
as if I am home again with my father
who forbade *wiri wiri* at the dinner table
who insisted on the first language of our family.

SMALL SHAME BLUES

I live with the small shame
of not knowing the multiple names for blue
to describe the nightsky over New Mexico
to describe the light in my lover's eyes.

It is a small shame that grows.

I live with the small shame
which resides in the absences of my speech
as I pause to search for the word in Spanish
to translate a poem to my Father
who sits there waiting
who scans my eyes to see
what I cannot fully describe
who waits for the word from me
the word that escapes me in the moment
the word I fear has never resided within me.

It is a small shame that grows
when indigo and cerulean are merely azul
and not *añil* and *cerúleo*.

Playing Scrabble with Cousin Fela

She insists if pax and discotheque are allowed
then so should *paz* and *discoteca*.

When she cannot find a single ñ
she declares the set defective.

She spends ten minutes arguing over *parkear*
and another twenty over *sangwiche*.

I try to explain to Fela that though
there are 40 million Latinos in the United States,
Spanglish isn't accepted in Scrabble.

She looks at me and says
I don't have the right tiles
to tell you what I think about escrabble.

2
The Trouble with Borders

Estoy norteada por todas las voces que me hablan
(*I am guided by all of the voices that speak to me*)
simultáneamente
(*simultaneously*)
—Gloria Anzaldúa, "A Struggle of Borders"

The Borders Are Fluid within Us

This is what is feared:
that flags do not nourish the blood,
that history is not glorious or truthful.

I sleep and dream in two languages.
I gain wisdom from more than one fountain.

I pass between borders
made to control what is owned.
The body cannot be owned.
The land cannot be owned,
only misunderstood or named by its knowing.

How the Land Longs to Be Loved

The earlier names are gone or mistranslated.
This is how a tribe becomes known
by a name it did not choose.
Like the Osage, whose song of a name
was transliterated by the French into a flatter chord,
to be transliterated by the English from the French
till you are left with two dull syllables
where there was once a melodious three
Wa-zha-zhe to Osage.

And yet the land still longs to be loved
by names that come slowly with time,
that hold our sense of understanding.
The older names have this charm
and so they last
and leak out
when the official ear least expects it.

Another generation goes searching for them
sifting through dust
through dictionaries of the obscure and archaic
for syllables that still tremble with the older meanings.

LAGO DE MIL OJOS

It stood near the lake of a thousand eyes,
in a valley of rattlesnake and scrub brush
where men worked all day in a cinder block hut
stopping each car between Laredo and Freer.

My father would roll down his window,
they would ask for his proof of identification,
he would smile and hand them his license,
they would ask questions, I would translate the answers.

How old was I when I recognized the interrogation
or understood the importance of my answers?
To be born here and never belong.
To fear the suspicion of authorities

Who might question the presence of a Cuban
in the middle of this desert,
who didn't speak the language,
who depended on a boy to tell his story.

To hold out one's card and one's perfect English,
to sit straight through their suspicions,
to pass muster and be waved through
to the lives we thought we had always known.

The Constant Agitation Over What Belongs

The honorable senator from Texas demands
to see the papers from the exotic invaders
who have been allowed for years
to swarm freely across the Gulf of Mexico.

He warns of invasion
and the spoiling of order.
He gesticulates his outrage
at the foreign-born menace.

The artilleries of defense are mustered
along fortifications of stone and chain.
But in the end the monarch butterflies
defeat the impossible borders of men.

When does what is strange become what is welcoming?
When exactly do we welcome what was once strange?

The honest answer is always yes
to what comes hidden in the hold of the ship
what is carried illicitly by the wind
what moves by its own motion
as any organism goes about free.

Queen Anne's Lace

Constellations on a slender stalk
how you have spread through the wind.
Brought by boat over oceans
seeded in the first gardens
who could contain you to a plot?
Once planted
remain where you are means nothing to a seed
or a weed
which is what they call you now
what we call what was never intended
by those who had no right to their intentions.

Now you grace the empty lots
of the cities of America
populate the cracks of green with your lacework
accompanied by the blue tongue of August
your consort chicory.

You were never part of any botanical plan
bishop's lace, wild carrot, zanahoria
all the names we give to your persistence.

Monarch Butterfly

They appear like pieces of orange gauze
the fluttering benedictions of the old goddess
Itzpapalotl the fearsome skeleton of bird and fire
that represented mothers who had died in childbirth.

They cross over land and water
from Isla Mujeres on the Yucatan
over strait to the Guanahacabibes of Cuba
to the phalangeal bones
of Cayo Hueso and North America.

Who can stop the insistence of butterflies
who pass from one generation to the next
through chrysalis and death
the cyclical routes of migration
that obeys a higher order
that flutters over serpentine rivers
and laughs at the false borders of men?

Nabokov Visits the Smithsonian

On the train to Washington
he remembered her little flit
and how she fluttered by
the walls of a western canyon.

Arriving he passed monuments
the tourists in their legislative domes
down the mall to the chambers of a trove
where he asked to see his fondest specimen.

There in the darkness she lay
wide open on its pin
neonymphas, his butterfly,
his greatest discovery and pride.

Here in the national vaults
it will transcend its dust
forever frozen in full flight
and marked by name and designation.

Leaving the city for another appointment
he thought nothing of the granite inscriptions
the statues to the heroes of importance
only the delicate traceries of her wing.

MR. GUZMAN MAKES A FOOL OF HIMSELF

He told me about traveling with the pickers
through the hot fields of Missouri and Iowa.
How when they got word they were coming
the people would run for the buses
while he emptied a bottle of whiskey over his head.

When the sheriff arrived he'd be found stumbling
alone in the field singing old rancheras they could not understand
ignoring the laughter of deputies
who'd throw him in jail to sober up while they called the Feds.

He said he'd take a nice long nap
and when he knew the buses were in the next county,
would stand up and yell,

Hey! Pendejos! I fought in the Korean War!
I'm a U.S. Citizen and I know my rights!
I'm entitled to my one phone call.

He always had a grin on his face
remembering the startled look of their faces.

3
THE TROUBLE WITH MEMORY

El alma emana, igual y eterna,
de los cuerpos diversos en forma y en color.
(The soul emanates, equal and eternal,
from bodies of diverse form and color.)
—José Martí

Norse Saga

Let us praise the immigrant
who leaves the tropics
and arrives in Chicago
in the dead of winter.

Let us praise the immigrant
who has never worn coats
who must bundle up
against an unimaginable cold.

For they will write letters home
that speak of it like Norse sagas
with claims that if a frigid hell exists
the entrance is hidden *somewhere* in this city.

Let us praise the immigrant
who fears the depths of the subway
the disappearance of landmarks
to guide them through the labyrinth.

Let us praise the immigrant
who dreams of the pleasures of sunstroke
who wakes each morning to the alien sight
of their breath suspended in the cold city air.

TIA FEFA IS A MENACE
TO THE CUBAN REVOLUTION

She would leave her family
her home and belongings
but Tia Fefa wouldn't leave everything
to the glorious Cuban Revolution.

And this is how Tia Fefa
went under anesthesia
allowing her dentist husband
to drill out her healthy molars.

It became a story in our family
"Tia Fefa and her Stealthy Molars"
which carried small treasure
past the airport security as they left.

Kept safe in the back of her mouth
off the island, all the way to Madrid
and then to the United States
where it allowed them to begin again.

In the first telling it was diamonds
then rubies and emeralds
until Tia Fefa's molars grew
to the size of refrigerator trucks.

She would leave her family
her home and belongings
but Tia Fefa wouldn't leave everything
to the glorious Cuban Revolution.

GOCHA

Arriving from Cuba three months after my birth,
she held me like treasure in those first photos,
sung me songs that had lulled my mother to sleep
and reminded me of geographies that preceded me.

In one photo the field is spread in bluebonnets
although the colors have now faded to white.
My grandmother is squinting in a painted dress
a half smile on her face in the bright Texas sun.

She is surrounded by flowers she does not know yet
in this alien country where her heart has taken her.
These are the native ornaments of the valley towns
where my grandfather ministered while she kept house.

He called her *Gocha* for Gloria
I called her *Lala* for the unpronounceable *Abuela*.
Two ways we modified the words that were proper
into the names by which she became known.

She taught me the flowers of her memory
blue *fausto* and *azulejo, majagua* and *flamboyán*.
In every garden she planted *camelia*,
tenacious reminder of all she left behind.

I have taken this new land inside of me
bluebonnet, western bluebell, heat's chicory
and plant *camelia* in my garden
to remind me of the geographies that preceded me.

The Interrogation of Poetry

I am home from college for the holidays
when my uncle subjects me to the interrogation
in which *What are you reading?* is followed
by *Do you understand what you are reading?*

It is the perfunctory questioning
from one generation to the next.
My reply that I am reading poetry
raises one eyebrow from the Spanish professor
who asks me for names.
I say, *I am mostly reading Neruda.*
Pablo Neruda? he asks.
I consider a joke about the Czech poet Jan Neruda
but think better and reply *Sí. Pablo Neruda.*

He is unable to stifle disbelief
and demands to see these books of Neruda.

So I go and return with
Elemental Odes and *Libro de Preguntas.*
He fingers each volume
inspects the Spanish against their translation
then asks *Do you understand them?*
I tell him I delight in them.

Then my uncle softens.
and tells me of his time as a student.
How Neruda was saved for the advanced courses
how he found him difficult to comprehend.

I didn't understand everything that was going on
but I knew there was something powerful
hidden beyond my comprehension.

My uncle never looked at me the same way again.

She Holds What Will Survive Her

These arms take the arms of years beyond her.
She holds close to her heart
which has kept time to the beat
of her lover
her babies
their babies
and now this rhythm
new to a world in need of a better beat.

This rhythm which now paces itself
to the metronomic teachings of her love.
She holds the child steady and close
transmitting to future generations her memory.

Beyond photograph what will he know of this?
That he was once held
in time
by time
that he was taught by touch
the older orders of love.

ARTIFACT

I was always confused by the photos
of my grandmother in Cuba.

In those pictures she looked older
than we knew her alive and among us.

I have seen the earliest one
when she was young and arresting.

In a white dress, she sits on an oil drum
with wild orchids in her hands.

She is as beautiful to the eye
as she would ever be allowed to be.

But in every other photo
she is weighted with the sadness

of a woman who was never asked,
who was never expected to know,

who always resided at the margins of men.

Hay Moros En La Costa

My father once threatened a dissolution
of the engagement,
the promise he made to my mother.
There were black rumors in her bloodline.
Assurances were made
the joining was consecrated
the story unfolded to me decades later.

The family would deny
the roots beneath the curly hair
the skin of the beloved grandfather
the histories of love that come creeping out to testify
to a past that cannot be dispossessed.

Grandfather of the suspect skin,
you are darker in all of the pictures,
and among the bare-headed brothers and nephews
I bear your hair
the rizado waves that flow when it grows long
reminders of the longer journeys of your blood.

But this is all mystery now.
They will not speak of it
the unthinkable meanings of being owned
the idea that property could produce progeny
that looks back and rights the record.

ABUELO

All of this comes to me through you.

You bore the name of Rodrigo de Triana
the shipmate on the voyages of Columbus,
the Sacajawea/John Smith of Spanish history books
who first sighted the continent
and guided the ships to land.

His life had such symmetry,
Triana for his town in Malaga
named for three Anas,
three women in the Bible.
Triana of the three women
who sailed the three ships,
named for three saints.
Believed to have been a Jew,
hiding as a Christian,
who converted to Islam late in life.

All of this comes to me through you, Abuelo.
The old religions and the misunderstandings
come all entwined through you.

Handsome Caudillos

Hatred as an element of the struggle; a relentless hatred of the enemy, impelling us over and beyond the natural limitations that man is heir to and transforming him into an effective, violent, selective and cold killing machine. Our soldiers must be thus; a people without hatred cannot vanquish a brutal enemy.

—Che Guevara

Tengo una remera del Che y no sé por qué,
I have a Che t-shirt and I don't know why.
  —Contemporary Argentine saying

I see the red shirt at the peace rally
and think of my parents
who left everyone and every
thing they knew and loved
save for the coin
forgotten in my brother's baby jacket.

Men like me in Cuba
failed the test of this symbol's manhood,
were called "Western perversions"
were imprisoned and made to labor.

Thousands, like these assembled,
were rounded up in the middle of the night
driven to the far countryside to cut sugarcane
for a revolution's economic quotas.

Tio Alberto's eyes go blank
when he speaks of the price he paid:
three years of forced hard labor
to work like a dog in the sun
for the privilege of leaving his own country.

I think of the chain of caudillos that promised
one thing and delivered another.

His Name Is Librado, Meaning "Freed"

He is an old man when I learn he was there
in the dark recesses of the new revolution's prison,
inherited from the deposed dictator,
who had inherited it from the conquistadores.
Now it was used for the secret tribunals
against the new state's old enemies.
Because new business cannot proceed before old business.

He was a young attorney providing ritual defense
to men who were doomed to only one verdict
from the sole jurist who had decided their fate
before they had entered the high walls of the fortress.

I see the judge's face often in crowds and demonstrations
on blood-red shirts of urban would-be *guerrilleros*.
Che is smiling and handsome—the very picture of certitude
whose details of excess have been excised by history,
the witnesses being dead or haunted by the sound
of executions occurring in the middle of the night.

My uncle's name is Librado, meaning "freed."
He carries within him stories that will not die.

CADÚCO

She wanted to see photos of my new home,
photos of my life with my new love.

But when I showed her the album
she said, *There are three of the two of you*
and the rest are of the dog.
I laughed and thought
Yes, this is what happens
when the tail grabs the heart.

Then my mother used a word
I'd never heard before.
You're cadúco, she said smiling.
What does that mean?
It means . . . and I could see her search for the translation,
You're gone.
There's no hope for you.
I still didn't get it.
Like you have gone over the waterfall.

And that's what it was alright.
I was securely in my barrel
smiling as I felt gravity give way.

MY DOUBLE

I tease you about the dog's affections.
You have his eye when you're in the room
and when you walk away his ears keep pace
in case his feet must follow.

He wants for you so dearly when you've departed.
I tell you, *What am I, chopped liver?*
But you are his beef bourguignon.
You are the steak tartare of his every dream.

I play green with envy
but the truth is, he is my clearest mirror.
If I lived in the lovetime of a dog
and thought that every time you left
you might not make it back
wouldn't I climb the chair near the window?
wouldn't I pace the floors in deep distress?

4
THE MEMORY OF THE TONGUE

By the rivers of Babylon, there we sat down,
yea, we wept, when we remembered Zion.
Psalm 137

Mamá Makes the Local Paper

Because Cuban food in South Texas
is like dishes from Venus or Mars,
a reporter is sent to interview Mamá.

She cribs the recipes from *Cocina Criolla*
and is photographed with her plates
in her nicest dress, and a bouffant
the size of her pressure cooker.

The reporter asks *Is it spicy?*
and betrays the fear
that if a name is accented
it will surely burn your tongue.
My mother demurs and reassures
that the spices we use are onion and garlic
but wisely withholds the amounts
which would undoubtedly alarm
the stomachs of Middle America.

It's 1974 and Corpus Christi, Texas
has never seen a thing like this.

Looking back at the newspaper clipping
my mother appears now as a pioneer.
Boldly she made the first *fricasé*
south of San Antonio,
the first *ajiaco*,
the first *ropa vieja*
and certainly the first *congrí*.

Where are the historical markers
to the persistence of cooks
who held fast to the old plates
who made flan in the new world?

MEMORIES OF THE LOST WORLD

Mojo criollo
Bustelo
Bijol
guarapo
mamey
malanga

I walk the aisles in Chicago and remember
the litany of all the things my parents longed for
when I was a child in South Texas.

This was before the Bering land bridge was built
between their memory and my understanding.

We would travel for miles on the rumor
that a market had opened
one that carried all the delights of their childhood.

Guava and bacalao are now plentiful in the supermarket
but seeing them still remind me of the years of desire and despair.
when my parents were strangers in a strange land
without the foods of profound belonging.

Garlic

The Mayan hieroglyph for garlic
is the shape of a starburst on the tongue.
It only appears with symbols
for human sacrifice and the afterlife.

It is said the Toltecs
only had one word for life
two words for death
but over a hundred words for garlic.

According to Bernardino de Sahagún
the name for the Aztec god of garlic
was so long and dangerous
pronouncing it would split
the speaker's tongue in two.

From this opening would sprout
a green vine with white blossoms of garlic
to season the celestial meats
of Omeyocan, the heaven of the gods.

ALLERGIES

There's rosemary, that's for remembrance.
—Shakespeare, *Hamlet*

I say I don't mind the allergy
if you have an excuse or a story.
It'll kill me passes muster,
or the story of why your mother hates rosemary.

She was young, times were lean
and her father came home with a skeletal rabbit
that had lived off nothing but pine.
The meal of it was the flavor of needles.

Her memory is why she hates the taste of rosemary.
But what I love even more is your father,
who hates rosemary for no memory
but for the love of his wife, your mother.

THE FORGOTTEN FRUIT OF CUBA

We are in the kitchen when
my parents begin speaking
of the forgotten fruit of Cuba.

Remember anón? asks Mama.
Una fruita blanca, says Papa.
Filled with tiny seeds my mother adds,
but nothing else in the world tastes like that.

The litany continues
guanabana, mamey, melocoton.

Melocoton? That's peach.
We have peaches I say and point to my yogurt.
But nothing like the peaches in Cuba, my mother says
and my father nods in agreement.

They stare at the plastic container
as I take another spoonful
of *melocotón* or *durazno* as the Mexicans call it
into this mouth that has never tasted
the forgotten fruit of Cuba.

Changri-la! my mother says.
Changri-la! my father repeats.

A far away look comes over their faces
as if their tongues have activated
a memory from a hundred years ago
perhaps from another dimension
that only exists in their dreams.

AMBROSIA ON FOUR LEGS

But He wanted something more exciting and said, "Enough. Let there be pork."
And there was pork—deep fried, whole roasted, pork rinds, and sausage.
                                                    —Richard Blanco, "Havanasis"

I tell my father they think it traveled on birds,

who flew across the Pacific and passed it to the pigs

  ¡Pobres puercitos! he says.

who then passed it along to the farmworkers

  ¡Pobres campesinos!

who then passed it along the line to some American tourists

  ¡Pobres turistas!

Mamá walks in and asks

  ¿Swiyen floo? ¿Que es eso?

Technically it's called H1N1 influenza.

  ¿Pero que es eso?!

Swine flu. Pigs. You can't eat any pork.

She looks at me and says

  I've lived long enough. I'll take my chances.

APPARITION

He was sleepy and really needed the coffee.
But when he lifted the cup to his lips
he could swear he saw
the face of Jesus smiling back at him.

Perhaps it was a morning hallucination.
But if the son of God appeared
  on a tortilla or a shower door,
He could certainly appear in his morning coffee.

With cup in hand, he thought of the call to the diocese,
imagined the flood of pilgrims to his door,
the clog of satellite trucks up and down the block,
while angry neighbors slammed doors on reporters.

But he was sleepy and really needed the coffee
so he took the apparition as benediction
and reached for the spoon.

Menu for an Immigrant Thanksgiving

We gave thanks with the cranberry
we who had never seen or tasted a cranberry
but we gave thanks with it nonetheless
ponquin pay tambien
we never saw it
or grew it
but it was there on the table
alongside the *guanajo*
that giant mass of Americano meat
which shared the oven with the priceless pig
which is what we really came for
Tio Alberto having prepared it for days
first over the slow coals of a backyard fire
before its final hours warmed beside the national bird.

When it was all done,
the alien mingled with the known,
we give thanks with the blessing of a custard flan
which has now disappeared into memory
with Tia Caruca
a flan that makes us all long for an afterlife
where she is still around to set her table
to make room for the dishes of two homes
the new and the remembered
to offer us limitless cups of *café cubano*
in the sleepy doldrums of heaven

5
THE GUIDE TO IMAGINARY MONUMENTS

Our own Greece is preferable
to the Greece that is not ours;
we need it more.
—José Martí

We'll start with the gold of Havana's women,
who hearing you needed money for your revolutionary war
offered their wedding rings and necklaces,
to be melted to finance
your white-wigged revolution
that was *so very bold*
but *so very poor.*
The skeleton of José Moñino y Redondo
has come to take it all back.
No muskets for you.
No cannons, no cannon balls,
no gunpowder, no bombs or mortars,
no clothes for your freezing soldier sons.
I'm afraid that bitter winter in Valley Forge
will end quite differently now.

While we're at it, we take back the help of our ancestors,
Bernardo de Galvez, Fernando de Leyba, and the thousands
of men with surnames that so displease you now,
who repelled the British in Florida and Louisiana,
who secured your flimsy Western borders
and marched to win your battles for you
in Indiana and Michigan and Missouri
before there was an Indiana or a Michigan, or a Missouri.

Hearing the commotion,
Francisco Saavédra de Sangronis has stirred in his Andalusian grave
demanding that while you're purifying the record
you return the half a million dollars in silver
that he collected in twenty-four hours
to fund your great final victory in Yorktown.

We will help you purify the record
but our ancestors insist on retroactively
removing themselves from your history.
And being a bit weak on your own history as you are
you may find the parting very hard to take.

Good Americans Organization, Circa 1952

Based on a photo in the Denver Public Library Archives.

This meeting of the Good Americans Organization
will now come to order.
We have gathered here
to calm your alarm.

Look how civil we are
how nicely we dress for you.
No sombreros or native dress.

Look! Here we have the American flag.
We know who won the wars,
who our grandparents signed the treaties with.
We swear allegiance to your history
and promise to make little trouble.

We will stop with our confounding tongue.
We will teach our children your language
so that their children will never understand us.
We will become the *abuelitos* who still speak the funny words
yet pronounce their last names with such finesse.

What we cannot do is make promises for the future,
for the ones that come after us,
or where their lingering hunger will lead them.

The Cuban Friendship Urn

The memory of the "Maine" will last forever
through the centuries as will the bonds of friendship
between Cuba and the United States of North America.
— Inscription on the Cuban Friendship Urn, Washington, DC

Graceful lines in relief
portray a goddess of liberty
beside the mast of the majestic ship
lying battered in the waters of Havana harbor.

This is the Cuban Friendship Urn
gift from the Machado government
to commemorate the ties that bound
and bind the memory of the sinking
that led to the war
that led to the liberation
that led to the occupation
that led to the revolution
that led to where we are.

Faraway from the prying eyes
of tourists to the capital city
or anyone who might discover
how friendship even etched in stone
can leave awkward silences in history.

This is why the urn
now stands majestically
beneath an overpass
beside a parking lot
behind Jefferson's enormous shoulder.

This is how we commemorate
the history of a friendship
between two nations
bound together irreparably
in the wreckage of history.

COMMEMORATIONS OF FORGOTTEN HISTORY

We are tired Cubans in the Catskills
standing by the side of the wooded road
outside of Haines Falls, New York.

We have come this far to see
the exact place where José Martí
wrote his *Simple Verses*.

The grand lodges of the leisure class are gone
the town the poet's doctor ordered him to
has largely disappeared into the dust.

Abuelo is upset to find no historical marker
no cognition in the eyes of the townspeople
who are oblivious to the sacredness of this spot.

Expecting statuary and murals
He is flabbergasted in disgust.
How can they not know Martí was here?

He is a romantic for the romantic
heroic for the heroic apostle of liberty.
Making peace of it, Abuela suggests we do it ourselves.

The falls that gave the name to this place
still flow under an arched bridge of stone
like the verses that bubble forth from his tongue.

Abuelo Antonio recites the *Simple Verses*,
commemorates where there is no commemoration,
marks the spot where a poet once wrote his simple song.

The Perils of the Monumental

This is not the postcard for the monument to J. Marion Sims
that lies in a leafy corner on the grounds
of the state capitol in Columbia, South Carolina.

That card would describe the graceful curve
of the marble line surrounding the niche
which holds the heroic bust
and the Hippocratic Oath
above the tributes to the father of gynecology.

On paper, as in stone,
no other names would appear,
no paean to Anarcha, Lucy, and Betsy,
the slaves who succumbed to his scalpel and speculum
no encomiums for the Irish destitute of New York
whose names were lost after his work was finished.

The engravers have packed up their own tools.
As if the stone cannot bear the true weight of that history.

José Dominguez, the First Latino in Outer Space

In that very first episode
the transmission is received on the starship Enterprise
that Space Commander Dominguez urgently needs his supplies.
Kirk tells Uhura to assure him
that the peppers are "prime Mexican reds
but he won't die if he goes a few more days without 'em."
Calm down Mexican.
You can wait a few more days to get your chile peppers.

In the corner of my eye I see Uhura's back hand twitch
and though I never see him on the screen
I image José giving Kirk a *soplamoco* to the face.

But this is the year 2266 and there are Latinos in Outer Space!
We never see them, but they've survived with their surnames
and their desire, deep in the farthest interplanetary reaches,
for a little heat to warm the bland food on the starbase at Corinth 4.
As it is on earth so it shall be in heaven.

Ricardo Montalbán will show up 21 episodes later
to play a crazy mutant *Indio*,
superhuman and supersmart
who survived two centuries
to slap Kirk around and take over his ship.

How La Lupe Defeated the Alien Invasion of 1969

In the end it was not a virus
or a cold that did them in.
It was the sound that came
from the upper registers of the radio dial.

For with all their strange alien skill they could not foretell
the dangers hidden in the weak AM radio signals
whose transmissions never pierced the Magellanic clouds.

They appeared and dispatched our planetary defenses
took the capitals of the vanquished governments
who prepared a ceremony of surrender.
Dignitaries came to submit and genuflect
till on the third day the ambassador of the Bronx
arrived to pay humble tribute in the form of his people's song.

The perpetual glowering grins of the alien representatives
flared when she appeared to serenade them.
La Lupe at the microphone began to move
and even with twelve eyes each, the strangers
could not detect how her body moved that day.
The devil in her body stirred that cadera shake
which caused their tentacles to feel their first perspiration
till by the third verse the delegation was writhing on the ground.

And then from the bodegas the swaying shocktroops arrived
armed with the hipsway threat of street corner tabletop armories
piled high with bootleg munitions of Celia Cruz and Tito Puente.

Within an hour Mongo Santamaria was blaring from open windows.
and Walter Cronkite gave way to Johnny Pacheco and the Fania All-Stars.
By the end of the day satellites in every orbit broadcast *guaracha* and *son montuno*
till every craft came tumbling down in quivering wrecks.

Nothing could have prepared the aliens when the trembling came
Traveling light years in the silence of deep space
had left them prone and unable to resist the corporeal quake.

But having no hips, they could not shake it off
and shattered themselves into oblivion.

Tall, Dark and Handsome Slums
in Gotham City

for Cesar Romero (1907–1994)

Beware the poison gas boutonniére
of an aging Latin heartthrob.
For I have covered my mustache in pancake
and traded pomade for green wig.

Cubans at 60 get no work in this town.
So I pull up my purple satin pants
button my yellow spats
and hold my head back for makeup.

The MGM contracts are gone.
No more Carmen Miranda in Havana.
No dancing with Betty Grable in the Rockies.
I've traded Marlene Dietrich for Catwoman.

My days may find me as Joker
but Butch the lothario eats on his own tab tonight.

ALL ORANGES AND BANANAS NOW

for Carmen Miranda (1909–1955)

Arriving in New York harbor she told the reporters
    I know plenty English words.
and five-fingered them off her hands
    Man. Man. Man. Man. Man. and
    Money. Money. Money. Money. Money.

Brazil's first *favela* music superstar and national export
was discovered singing *samba* in hats of her own making
and with her hipsway work brought color and motion
to Broadway and then the movie screens of a world lost in depression,
And so became the highest paid actress of her era.

For thirty years she stirred the blood of Middle America,
till in that grainy footage she appears:
Red Skelton speaks her name and the studio audience goes wild.
Carmen appears with arms outstretched
a sequined cornucopia in high heels that shakes
and then careens to a jerk before her final fall.

Maria do Carmo would never be seen again
and in a week the streets of Rio would swell to mourn
the little girl milliner made international icon of delight.

Today she is distilled to fruited hat, arching brows and almond eyes
on the label of every yellow bunch.
While in the movies she remains the first Latin goddess
at the center of Busby Berkeley constellations,
singing to a country that never quite understands.

Asombrado

The 2009 March on Washington for Immigration Reform

Nothing beats the surprise
on the faces of daily commuters
who looked on in disbelief
in every metro car in Washington.

The faces are baffled and alarmed
to see the ocean of accented voices
which swelled from the suburbs
of Maryland and Virginia
through the subterranean labyrinths
to rise in the heart of the capital city.

They march past the office buildings
of the government that can not see them
that considers them a menace and urban legend.

When they reach the national mall
a smile appears on every face
as if they have arrived to the knowledge
of who they are and where they are standing.

There between the capitol and the monuments
a ripple of comprehension takes hold
and the dream unfurls again.

BIOGRAPHICAL NOTE

Dan Vera is a writer, editor and literary historian living in Washington, DC. He is the author of the poetry collection *The Space Between Our Danger and Delight* (Beothuk Books, 2008), and the editor of the gay culture journal *White Crane*. His poetry has appeared in various journals including *Beltway Poetry, Cutthroat, Delaware Poetry Review, Gargoyle, Little Patuxent Review, Naugatuck River, Notre Dame Review,* as well as the anthologies *Divining Divas, DC, DC Poets Against the War* and *Full Moon On K Street: Poems About Washington*. He's the co-creator of the literary history site, DC Writers' Homes, and chairs the board of Split This Rock Poetry.

Printed in the USA
CPSIA information can be obtained
at www.ICGtesting.com
JSHW082224140824
68134JS00015B/731

9 781597 092746